GERBILS
AS A NEW PET

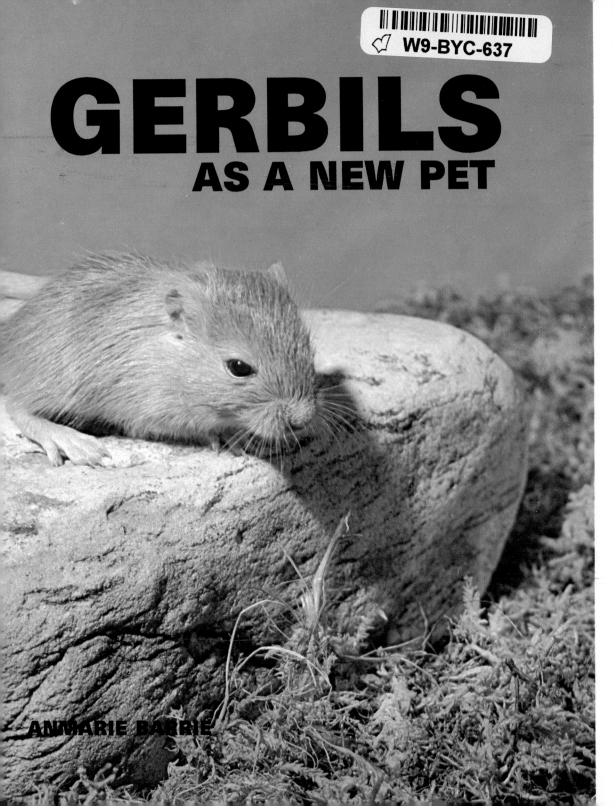

ANMARIE BARRIE

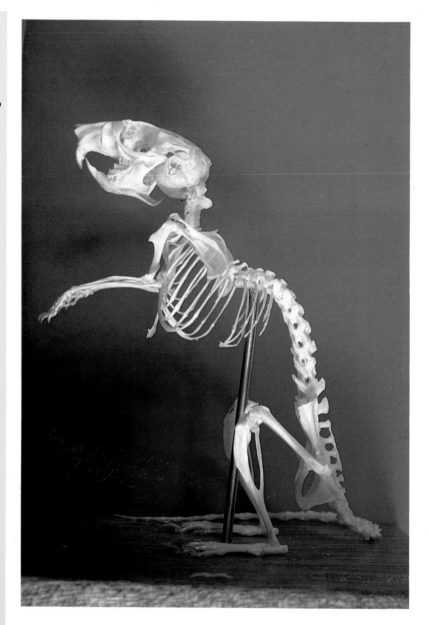

Skeleton of a gerbil. Photo by Dr. Herbert R. Axelrod.

Introduction

Although the gerbil or jird is a pet of comparatively recent popularity, having first been introduced to the pet-loving public in the 1960's, it has established itself quite firmly alongside the more popular hamster. The hamster is still, however, the most popular rodent, but the gerbil's increasing recognition may someday offer competition.

This is not surprising. Gerbils have some wonderful attributes: they consume little food, their accommodations require minimum space, they are hardy animals, have little odor, are prolific breeders, and rarely, if ever, bite.

Additionally, gerbils come in a wide assortment of colors, with more varieties sure to appear in the future. So although most gerbils are kept as pets by children, many adults find it challenging to breed and exhibit these little rodents. This is a wonderful aspect of the hobby; the entire family can join in, share, and enjoy a common interest.

Gerbils have a further advantage over many pets; they are inexpensive to purchase and maintain.

Unlike hamsters, gerbils should not be kept as single pets. Gerbils are social creatures who enjoy their own kind. They should be kept in small groups.

Gerbils have a good lifespan for such a small animal. They may attain five or more years of age.

Black gerbil eating lettuce. Wild gerbils eat almost any vegetable matter that man eats.

3

Natural History

There are about 80 species of gerbils in the wild. They are found in an extensive area of distribution stretching from China and Mongolia, through Asia and into Africa. The popular pet we know is scientifically referred to as *Meriones meridianus,* the South Mongolian jird, or *Meriones unguiculatus,* the clawed jird, also from Mongolia.

Gerbils are nocturnal creatures. This means they are active at night. Most species, though, will venture forth during the daylight hours.

ORIGIN OF NAME

The word gerbil is derived from the generic name for these animals, *Gerbillus.* This in turn is derived from the Arabic word jarbu, meaning rodent, and the Latin illus, meaning small. *Meriones* is a mythological man who fought in the Trojan wars of Greece. *Meridianus* is Latin for midday. Pet gerbils are referred to by zoologists as jirds, from the Berber word gherda.

Most scientific names for animals are of Latin or Greek origin, to which French and other language derivatives have been added. The reason for this is that the system used to classify animals was developed by Carl von Linne, a Swedish naturalist and scholar. Latin was the standard language for all scholars of his time. Latin also had the advantage of being a defunct language. Thus it was acceptable to people of all nations. Linne used a binomial system of nomenclature in his system of taxonomy. He gave each animal two names. The first is the generic name, the second the specific name. When both generic and specific names are used together, a species is identified. No two species have the same combination of two names. It is customary to differentiate the scientific taxonomic names from the rest of the text in a book or article. This is why such names appear in italics.

Just as all like species are

placed in genera, so all similar genera are placed in larger groups called families. Based on similarities, the groups become larger and the class Mammalia—those animals which have hair, suckle their young, and are born alive. Rodentia is the largest of all mammalian

The Greater Egyptian Gerbil, *Gerbillus pyramidum.* These gerbils have never become as popular as the Mongolian Gerbil.

larger, referred to as orders, classes and phyla respectively. The grouping ends with all animal forms placed in the kingdom Animalia. Together with the kingdom of plants, these two groups encompass all life as we know it.

RODENTS

The gerbil is a member of the order Rodentia. This order is one of 17 making up orders, containing 1,800 or more groups.

The term rodent is derived from *rodo,* Latin for gnaw. The word gives a clue to this group of animals. All rodents share a common characteristic: the front teeth, known as incisors, grow continually. The incisors can be maintained only by constant gnawing to trim the edges. The two upper incisors overlap and

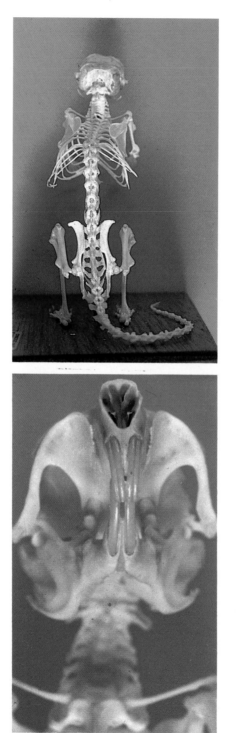

This back view of a gerbil's skelton shows how the tail and backbone are connected. They have the same kind of bones.

A front view of the head shows a huge nostril opening. The two upper incisors overlapping and just touching the lower incisors. Constant gnawing is required to keep the incisors ground down or they will grow and grow until the poor animal is unable to eat.

just touch the two below to effect an efficient chiseling action.

Mice, rats, hamsters, guinea pigs, agoutis, and chinchillas are all rodents. Surprisingly, rabbits are not. They are grouped in a related order called *Lagomorpha.*

ADAPTATION

Rodents are adaptable to new habitats to such a degree that man has found them already living where he has ventured, or if not, they were transported with him and thrived. Rats and mice in particular have shown their ability to succeed. Rodents consume more seed grown in America than the total amount of seed exported to other countries.

Rodents are able to gnaw through telephone cables, concrete, wood, and even thin metal. They can survive in deserts, frozen wastes, the tropics, in trees, on river banks, and throughout buildings. They run swiftly, jump, and swim. Some even glide considerable distances.

Many rodents, especially the smaller ones, can subsist on an amazingly sparse diet. They eat wood, paper, cloth, and other items not fit for many animals. Some species can live on very little water. In addition, they have the ability to reproduce prolifically. Indeed rodents are very successful animals. Their numbers are kept in check by man and a multitude of other predators, including snakes, lizards, hawks, owls, foxes, cats, wolves, and wild dogs.

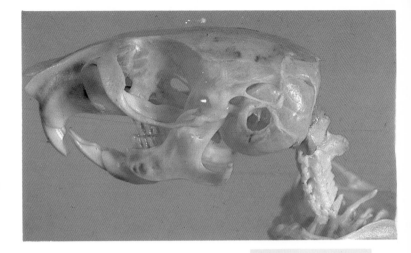

GERBILLINAE

Rodents of the suborder Myomorpha are divided into nine families. The cricetid rodents (family Cricetidae) are our prime concern. This family consists of five subfamilies, one of which is Gerbillinae, containing all gerbils.

Most gerbils are similar to each other. Only two types may be considered different from the average. The most obvious of these is the fat-tailed mouse, *Pachyuromys duprasi*. It has a stout tail capable of containing a large amount of food which has been converted into fatty tissue. The animal can live off this when times are hard—a useful adaptation for survival for an animal living in a desert.

The other different gerbil is the great gerbil (*Rhombomys opimus*). This creature lives in the semi-deserts of Mongolia, China, and Turkestan. This 36 cm (14 in) species is diurnal, meaning that it's active in the daytime. This is unusual for a gerbil.

DESCRIPTION

All gerbils follow much the same pattern of conformation. They are mouse or rat-like in appearance but have longer rear legs enabling them to jump and hop. Body size varies from as little as 8 cm (3 in) to about 19 cm (7½ in) in most species. The great gerbil is an exception to this. The gerbils of the genus *Meriones* are generally 20-30

A side view of the head of a gerbil showing how strong the incisors are. All skeletal photos by Dr. Herbert R. Axelrod.

7

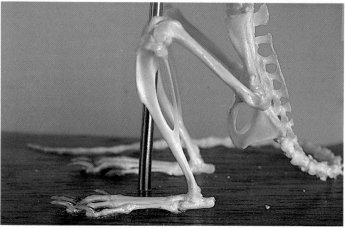

Body color is usually sandy brown with gray and black ticking, producing an agouti type pattern. The underbelly fur is normally a lighter color, almost white, depending on the species. The ears are of moderate size in pet gerbils, while those of the small wild species appear larger in proportion to head size. The pointed snout bears whiskers. The eyes are somewhat large as befits a nocturnal species. The tail is covered with hair in all species, more in some than

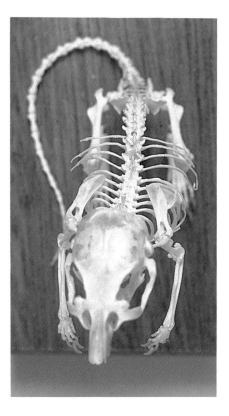

Top view from the head down to show the claws with a hand (paw) amazingly like a human's. The legs show the split bone, which is very unhumanlike. The photo to the right is a general top view of a gerbil's skeleton.

cm (7¾—11¾ in) in length. Typical tail length ranges from 7.5 cm (2¾ in) to 19 cm (7½ in). In the large gerbils of the genus *Tatera*, the tail can reach 25 cm (9¾ in). An average adult weight is 50-75 gm (1¾—2½ oz.) Females are ordinarily somewhat heavier than males. Most pet gerbils are toward the lower limits of the averages stated.

others. Most tails also have bushy tips, but this feature is not seen as strikingly in pets as in wild species. Gerbils can shed their tails in an emergency. However, the tail will not regrow to its former length once shed.

LIFE IN THE WILD

Life for a wild gerbil is not easy. It must contend with harsh living conditions and be ever watchful of natural enemies. Although large numbers of baby gerbils are born each year, the greater number of these are killed by predators. Only a few live beyond their first year of age. Nonetheless, enough survive so that colonies continually grow. Many colonies will live in close proximity to each other.

Gerbils live in underground tunnels. The tunnel may be comprised of a main channel with just one or two side pockets, or it may be a highly complex unit with interconnecting passages forming a labyrinth. The entrance holes are usually very small (just large enough for the gerbils to

The Small Naked-soled Gerbil, *Taterillus emini,* **is found ranging in the desert areas of East Africa. They are nocturnal because they would desiccate in the hot sun of the desert.**

9

enter); often they are sealed during the daytime.

A typical colony contains a male, several females, and offspring of varying ages. Very large colonies house many males and females living as smaller units within the one large underground maze of tunnels and dens.

Theoretically, it would be expected that wild gerbils would be closely inbred given their colony lifestyle. Nature has devised a way of avoiding this. It is believed that females leave their own colonies to mate in others nearby. After mating, they return to their own colony to bear the young. This keeps the degree of inbreeding down to acceptable levels.

Gerbils are quite cosmopolitan in their feeding habits. This is a prerequisite for desert living. Gerbils will eat shoots, leaves, seed, and the like; they also eat insects, grubs, and worms. One species, the large Indian gerbil, *Tatera indicus,* is known to take the eggs and young of birds.

Gerbils are especially adapted to survive without water for long periods. This is achieved by digestive tract

A Small Naked-soled Gerbil female with her youngster, out at night, searching for food. Though they prefer grain, they will also eat insects, like this Jewel Beetle it is sniffing.

modifications: the kidneys operate at maximum efficiency in retaining water; urination is less regular, and fecal pellets are made less moist.

PETSHOP GERBILS

Gerbils seen in petshops are commonly of the genus *Meriones*. There are about ten or twelve species in this taxon. Occasionally, a gerbil is displayed from another genera, but these specimens are often more expensive. Their care and accommodations are basically the same, with allowance made for those animals of larger size.

Also requiring similar treatment are the various species of jumping mice and jerboas of the families Zapodidae and Dipodidae. Many of these hail from habitats similar to the gerbils'. Others are from more temperate regions, such as North America, and have more specialized feeding habits. Should you see gerbil-like animals for sale, check out exactly what they are so they can be cared for accordingly.

This gray gerbil is munching on dried seeds, a favorite diet. As more people breed gerbils, more color varieties appear amongst the offspring. Color mutants are a mathematical probability, but only when large numbers are involved. Photo by M. Gilroy.

Color Forms

Compared to the rabbit or guinea pig, the gerbil is still in its infancy when considering the development of varieties. Presently there are about ten different colors available. This means that there is plenty of scope for the enthusiastic breeder. No doubt there will be an increase in the number of colors and coat types.

It is not possible to hurry new colors or change coat textures. These traits are dependent on mutations happening within gerbils. A mutation is the sudden change in the way a gene expresses itself. Once mutated, the gene of the mutated feature is passed on to a gerbil's offspring. By selectively breeding these offspring, it is possible to increase the incidence of the mutation in the population as a whole. However, this takes a lot of time.

A mutation can happen at any time, in anyone's stock. A mutation is not dependent on the quality of stock. It often happens that the quality of type is not as good in the latest colors as it was in the original colors or earlier mutations. Once a new color is well-established, it is possible to be more particular about type. (Type refers to a gerbil's overall conformation to the ideals laid down by gerbil societies.)

Once mutations of color genes have taken place in a species, it is possible to create new colors by recombining the mutations. This progressively growing

A closeup of the skeletal tail of a gerbil. Besides using it for balance, the gerbil stores energy in the form of fat in its tail. It may shed its tail during combat or under attack by predators, but the tail does not regenerate. Photo by Dr. Herbert R. Axelrod.

aspect of the hobby attracts many specialty breeders whose main interest is developing colors. Other breeders specialize in improving type. Most enthusiasts dabble in breeding for the pure enjoyment of the hobby, regardless of the color or variety involved.

darker tip of bushy hairs on the tip. The ears should be short and erect. The eyes must be large, yet not bulge. A circle of gray hairs around the eyes is ideal. The nails should be black. The overall color is a reddish brown.

The coloring of the nails is,

An agouti-colored gerbil. This is the natural color of the wild gerbil.

AGOUTI

The agouti is the oldest form. A good exhibition gerbil should have a clear line of demarcation between the agouti color on the back and sides and that of the paler (usually white) underbelly. The skin should be grayish in color. The tail should be darker on its upper surface with an even

however, subject to a degree of variation. In wild populations, this variation is a genetic essential. Wild gerbils reflect the type of area in which they live. Those from hot desert climates are usually lighter-colored than those from cooler regions.

A gerbil without ticking in its fur is called a dilute. There is also a gray-bellied form of both the normal and dilute colors.

CANADIAN WHITE SPOT

The first gerbil mutation occurred in Canada in the late 1960s. An ideal specimen has two clear white spots, one on the crown of the head and the other on the back of the neck. The single white spot, or simply white spot, has just the mark on the crown.

This white spot mutation has been transferred to the other colors, but not always as a spot. In some gerbils, it appears in irregular patches of white. This mutation undoubtedly will be reinforced to create even larger patches.

DARK-TAILED WHITE

The first dark-tailed whites were considered to be albinos. A number of people today still call any all-white animal an albino. This holds true only if the animal is totally devoid of melanin pigment, in which case the eyes typically are red. The dark-tailed white gerbil shows darker hairs on its tail as it matures; thus, it is not a true albino.

However, an albino mutation has now appeared. It is likely that a Himalayan variety will follow, for this is normally found at the albino locus of the color genes.

BLACK

The appearance of the black mutation came during the late 1970s. It was produced in the USAF

Two red-eyed gerbils. The albino is the red-eyed white gerbil.

A magnificent specimen of a Canadian White Spot Gerbil showing the clear white spot on the crown of the head and the other on the back of the neck. Photo by Michael Gilroy.

Aerospace Laboratories in Texas. As expected, it appeared from agouti parents. This mutation opened up numerous future potential colors.

The black should contain no white hairs. This is not easy to achieve, as exhibited

by the many black specimens carrying white hairs. Selective breeding for black will however result in a steady improvement of the color.

ARGENTE

The argente mutation is of British origin. It is a dilution of the agouti gene and a very attractive color. Rabbit fanciers might be surprised to find it was not, in fact, a true argente color (which is

silver), but more of a light golden shade in which gray hairs are found. Certainly the use of argente is misleading as a descriptive color. The overall color is produced by the fact that each of the component colors of the agouti (yellow, brown, and black) are weakened in their intensity. Argente gerbils have red eyes.

LILAC

The lilac gerbil is a grayish brown, resulting from the paling effect created by crossing argente with black. This will produce agoutis of various types. The lilac is achieved by selecting the light-colored examples. The eye color is red.

BLUE

This is one of the new colors. It is produced by a dilution effect on the black coloration. The blue has the same problem as the black—it often carries white hairs. Another problem is that there may be a brown cast to the color, also similar to when the black is diluted. Blue gerbils will improve their color with age, but it will be difficult because a truly identifiable shade of

A gray agouti. This is a rare gerbil color. Photo by Michael Gilroy.

blue can simply look like a washed out black. The eye color is black.

CREAM

The cream is really a dilution of the argente, produced by breeding to the red-eyed whites. Here the line of demarcation between body and underbelly may not be evident at all, or barely so, depending on the shade achieved. In due course, black-eyed creams, as opposed to the red-eyed ones, will be available.

GRAY AGOUTI

The gray agouti is yet another dilution. The black is diluted to blue while the red and brown are likewise reduced. It has been called chinchilla, but this may not be correct. The extent of dilution of the red color in the chinchilla is almost total, thus reducing it to white.

THE FUTURE

There is no doubt that patterned gerbils will appear in the coming years. This will herald an exciting period for breeders. The thoughts of a banded or Dutch-marked gerbil are thrilling.

Roans, magpies, black and
tan, fox-marked, and many
more are all possibilities. It
may well be that you will be
one of the pioneers in this
hobby.

From top to
bottom, the four
gerbils are an
albino, a dove, a
cinnam on and
an agouti. Photos
by Michael
Gilroy.

Accommodations

The essentials of a good home are that it is spacious, escape-proof, easy to clean, and loaded with useful items for a gerbil. Within these parameters, there is considerable scope to use your imagination to provide a home in which your gerbils will be at their best.

One of the main considerations with many small rodents, such as hamsters and gerbils, is that they are nocturnal creatures.

Their home should reflect the fact that they prefer to sleep in a darkened area.

Gerbil accommodations come in a great many sizes. Offer your pets the largest quality home you can afford and comfortably accommodate.

METAL CAGES

The typical metal cage is a box shape constructed of wire bars. These are usually designed to be taken apart

A child feeding her gerbils some lettuce. The plastic aquarium/terrarium is not ideally suited for housing gerbils, as it tips easily and it is possible the gerbils can climb atop one another and escape.

readily for easy cleaning. A small raised ledge along one wall, a nesting box, or an exercise wheel may be within the cage. One without a wheel is preferred. Gerbils, unlike hamsters, have a long tail which can get caught in the open treads. A gerbil wheel should be solid and fitted to the side of a cage so the gerbil is in no danger.

Metal cages do not soak up urine, but they can be easily wiped clean. The wire fronts and tops should fit neatly into place. There should be no sharp edges and no exposed gaps through which a gerbil can escape. If the cage is painted, check that the paintwork is of good quality. Once the paint starts to peel, the metal quickly rusts. This is a source of bacterial activity, so repaint or replace the cage quickly.

METAL AND PLASTIC

A popular cage today has all wire top and sides clipped onto a plastic base. These are easy to maintain and the base cannot rust. Be sure there are no protruding pieces of plastic on which a gerbil can gnaw, as they can rapidly be made into an escape hole.

The bars on these

commercial cages are normally chromium-plated. Check the plating to ensure it has been done well.

ALL PLASTIC TUBES

There is a housing system on the market that reflects the nature of many rodents. It is comprised of large plastic drums to which plastic tubes and smaller drums attach to create a series of tunnels and dens. Such a system can be used by itself, or parts can be used to enhance other gerbil housing.

AQUARIUMS

A sizeable aquarium tank provides a good home for gerbils. The aquarium is easy to clean and will not rust. The tank can be either

You can grow your own greens for your gerbil. Pet shops sell greenhouse kits that provide everything you need to grow fresh organic greens. Photo courtesy of Four Paws.

21

This series of photos shows a mother Argente-colored gerbil with her Argente baby. They live in the tube. The mother passes food to her baby and very easily accesses the tube herself using her tail as a fifth leg. Photos by Michael Gilroy.

of plastic (Plexiglass) or glass. The latter is more expensive but has a greater life potential. Some petshops sell leaky tanks at low prices. These will work fine. Place a cover of welded wire mesh on the top so the gerbils cannot jump out.

FLOOR COVERING

There are a number of floor coverings available. The final choice is one of personal preference.

Sawdust: This should come from wood that has not been treated with chemicals that might be toxic to a gerbil. White sawdust is preferred because it will not stain an animal's coat. The advantage of sawdust is that it soaks up urine quickly; however, it tends to cling to fur, fruit and anything damp. Sawdust can also irritate eyes, as it tends to produce more dust than other options.

Wood Shavings: These do not soak up urine or spilt water as well as sawdust, but they do not cling as badly to fur and food.

Shredded Paper: There are a variety of commercially shredded papers available

which soak up liquids rather well. They are not dangerous if swallowed by the animals, either. Granulated forms are also on the market, but they are a bit more expensive.

Sand: Few people use sand. They fear it will stain a gerbil's light underfur, or don't appreciate it because it may get kicked out of the cage as gerbils play in it. Sand is best when used in a sealed unit, such as a fish tank, where the gerbils' motion will not result in sand being scattered outside of their environment.

BEDDING MATERIAL

The average gerbil likes to make a nest. The selection of

This old-style aquarium is satisfactory but the gerbil will almost certainly chew on the cement holding the glass in place. This cement might be toxic. This particular dog is friendly to the gerbils. Normally dogs and cats kill gerbils instinctively. Photo by Paul Bartley.

23

bedding material is extensive. Good quality meadow hay is a popular

choice, but watch that it does not become damp in the nest. This increases the risk of mold or other spores finding a safe haven in which to breed. Strips of paper towels are also appreciated. These need only be placed near the nesting compartment. The gerbils will shred them to the desired size and take them into the sleeping quarters.

Dried leaves are another natural bedding material, as are many types of dried plants. Ensure that these materials are not poisonous to your gerbils. Avoid items such as wool, cotton from spools, manufactured packing material, nylon shreds, or any other material that a gerbil can swallow or get tangled around its neck.

FEEDING UTENSILS

There are many feeding pots suitable for gerbils. The best are bottom–heavy, earthenware bowls, for they cannot be tipped over easily.

Water can also be supplied via open pots. However, these soon become contaminated with floor material, food, and feces. Inverted, gravity feed bottles are a better choice. These clip on to the sides of the cage. A gerbil gets its fill of water by licking at a metal spout. Do not purchase a water bottle with a plastic or glass drinking tube. Glass shatters and plastic is destroyed by constant gnawing.

There are grooming tools specially designed for small animals such as gerbils. Regularly grooming your pet will help keep its coat looking nice and healthy. Photo courtesy of Four Paws.

CAGE FURNISHINGS

Gerbils are intelligent and inquisitive animals. Gerbils are good at inventing their own games, yet they need a number of items that are both entertaining and safe. Avoid anything made of plastic which can be chewed and eaten.

Given their need to gnaw, pieces of wood are always a favorite with gerbils. Fruit tree branches, thread bobbins, and pine cones are sources of amusement.

In larger cages, empty jars weighted with some pebbles are of interest, as are cardboard tubes from paper towels. A small bedding area can be sculpted from concrete and plaster to look like a cave. You may be tempted to build bigger and more unique accommodations as you let your imagination take control.

CLEANING

Regardless of the size of your pets' home, it must be cleaned on a regular basis.

An inverted, gravity-fed waterer. The gerbil gets water when it licks the bottom of the spout.

Screen covers are probably the most sensible tank tops you can use with gerbils being kept in glass enclosures. Photo courtesy of Four Paws.

Once a week is average, but it may be necessary more often, depending on the number of gerbils living in the home. All feeding utensils should be washed daily. Clean the home and its accessories with a mild, diluted disinfectant. The cage, the accessories, and all utensils must be thoroughly rinsed and dried before reintroducing them to your gerbils.

From top to bottom: two females, a cinnamon and a sable, live together very happily. Males may be troublesome if kept with females. In the center is an Argente (silver) with its almost fully grown baby. Below: A fully grown young Argente which shows the silver hairs covering most of its belly region too. Photos by Michael Gilroy.

Selecting Stock

There are a number of aspects to consider when selecting stock. Initially, decide whether your gerbil is required simply as a pet or for breeding and exhibition. A petshop has many gerbils available as delightful companions. However, a gerbil required for breeding and exhibition should be selected with more discrimination. A gerbil of good quality and known history is required.

The petshop will probably put the gerbil into a small box for you to bring it home. Gerbils have been known to chew their way out of such confinement so the less time spent there, the better. The housing and accessories should be set up even before you bring your pet home. This way you won't have to buy housing and equipment on the spot when you select your gerbil. You can buy accommodations suitable to your needs and pocketbook.

AGE

Acquire a gerbil that is young so that it can be tamed. Remember that gerbils have a lifespan of only four or five years. The ideal age at which to purchase a gerbil is when it is about four weeks old; at this time, it will be weaned and eating independently of its mother.

While a youngster, a gerbil can be introduced to other young gerbils without risk of serious fighting. Older animals need careful supervision initially as they become familiar with one another. It is best if gerbils that are strangers to one

Acquire your pet gerbil as young as you can. The young are easier to tame and become much friendlier. Photo by Dr. Herbert R. Axelrod.

another are introduced to their quarters at the same time. This gives both animals something new to explore without either pet having an "in-house" advantage.

NON-BREEDING PETS

If you do not plan to breed your pets, purchase only females. They will live in better harmony than males. Males can coexist, but only if introduced to one another at an early age. Even then fighting is likely to break out. Having pets of the same sex prevents unwanted matings.

A key factor in keeping peace, even if the animals are of a social nature, is space availability. The less space available, the more likely fighting will become serious, for the inhabitants are not able to keep out of one another's way. Another factor is solidarity, for once a group of gerbils has established a colony, it is difficult to introduce newcomers. The residents perceive an unfamiliar gerbil as an intruder and attack it.

HEALTH

The most important concern when selecting any pet is its health. Avoid a gerbil that appears lethargic or has difficulty moving

Healthy gerbils are active gerbils. It is natural for the gerbil to climb and be inquisitive. If the gerbil you have merely hides in one spot, there is probably something wrong with it healthwise. This is a cinnamon-colored gerbil.

about. Indeed, reject all specimens that appear less than fit in any way, for they may be suffering from an ailment or disorder.

Observe the prospective gerbils for a few moments. Select one that catches your attention. The eyes should be round and clear. The ears must be erect, with no sign of pieces missing as a result of fighting. The nose should be free of discharge. The fur should be sleek. The body should be free of bald patches, sores, or any evidence of parasites. All five digits should be present on each foot. The tail should be straight and complete. No fecal droppings or stained fur should be apparent around the anus.

Glance into the cage; every gerbil should be fit. If one appears ill, its cagemates may be infected. The petshop itself should be clean, tidy, and well stocked. The cages of all the animals should be well kept and their occupants in sound condition. Such a store knows how to care for its animals. Here you can purchase your pet, the necessary equipment, and ask for advice. Make your purchase only when you are fully satisfied.

HANDLING

Gerbils are fast moving animals, which makes handling a bit of a challenge at first, especially with the young which tend to be quite small.

It is important not to frighten a gerbil. Movements near the cage should be slow. Approach the cage from the front so the animals can see you. Cup your hands so that a gerbil is contained within. Use one hand to take hold of the tail, not the tip. Now gently slide the other hand under the gerbil's body to support its weight. Restrict

handling to just this state until the gerbil is more comfortable to your touch.

PRECAUTIONS

Never allow a gerbil out of its cage when there are cats or dogs around. Even a playful nip can bring tragedy to your gerbil. Other potential hazards include an exploring gerbil vanishing into cracks and crevices, or jumping from a high place to the floor and injuring itself. Young children must be supervised when handling gerbils. Teach them the correct way to lift and handle a gerbil. A room must be gerbil-proofed before you let the animal explore!

BREEDING STOCK

Visit a number of small animal exhibitions to become familiar with gerbil standards. Discuss your interest with breeders and dealers so you can select fine specimens and sound accommodations. Plan ahead. Breeding requires time, money, and space. Also, know ahead of time what will be done with the offspring and make the necessary arrangements.

A suitable trio is a good

start. Do not bargain-hunt! The idea behind breeding is to strive to improve stock, not to breed inferior stock. Do not commence with too large a breeding stock; first you need to gain experience with breeding pairs and raising young. You do not want to become overrun with gerbils for which you cannot find homes. Begin in a small way and build on your experience.

It may be fun to let your gerbils play outside the cage, but once they become free, they quickly revert to their wild habits and can become a nuisance...like mice. Photo by Bob Bernhard.

An albino and an agouti gerbil. Breeders use cages made of plastic like those shown in the background.

Feeding

All rodents are easy to feed. Gerbils are no exception. These animals can survive on spartan diets in the wild. Captive gerbils are far healthier than their wild counterparts because a wide variety of foods is available to them. Such variety increases their resistance to disease and enables them to bear and raise young with less difficulty.

FOOD GROUPS

All foods fall into one of two broad groups: those rich in carbohydrates, and those rich in fatty oils and proteins. Both types, together with water, are essential to healthy growth. Foods are processed in the body to provide energy and tissue replacement. For these functions to occur, an animal needs various vitamins and minerals. These substances are found in foods in differing ratios. This explains the necessity of a varied diet.

CEREALS

The basic diet of most rodents is cereal. Cereals are rich in carbohydrates. Carbohydrates provide energy for muscular activity. Any carbohydrates (sugars and starches) surplus to a gerbil's needs are broken down into simple sugars which are converted into fatty material. This material is then stored in the body to provide insulation and an energy reserve.

The popular cereals are crushed oats, wheat, barley, maize, rye, and the various products made from these: corn flakes, bran, porridge, and shredded wheat, etc. Wholemeal bread, baked bread, dog biscuits, and cookies are other sources of carbohydrates which appeal to gerbils.

Ready-mixed packets of gerbil food can be purchased from your local petshop. An alternative is to buy the various cereals in individual lots and make your own mix based on the preferences of your stock. The important consideration, whichever the method you choose, is to ensure that all food fed to your pets is clean and fresh. It should not be stored where there is a risk of its being fouled by wild rodents. It must also be stored in a

Gerbils are rodents, like rats and mice. They are very easy to feed, but they prefer grains of cereals which are rich in carbohydrates and have lots of water. Photo by Michael Gilroy.

dry area; dampness encourages the growth of mold.

stored in concentrated amounts. Most of the seeds supplied to cage birds will be

Popular Cereal Constituents by %			
Cereal	Carbohydrate	Fat/Protein	Mineral
Wheat	74	13	2
Barley	70	12	2
Maize	63	17	2
Oats	56	16	2

PROTEINS AND FATS

Proteins are found in both plant and animal tissues. They are composed of amino acids. Proteins are required for the building of muscle and to replace tissues that become worn out or damaged. Excess protein is converted into fats. This excess is laid down in the tissues to provide insulation and energy reserves.

Fats serve a few roles in the body apart from insulation. They assist in the assimilation of proteins and carbohydrates. They also represent easily available sugars if broken down by oxidization in the body. Food rich in protein is typically well-supplied with fat.

Generally, most of the proteins needed by a gerbil are obtained from the seeds of plants. Here proteins are

taken by gerbils, as will many types of nuts. Those that your pets seem particularly fond of can be given as treats.

A healthy treat is soaked seed. The reason is that the protein and vitamin content of the seed rises dramatically. Simply soak some fresh seed in warm water for 12 hours. This triggers the germination process. Rinse the seed and store in a warm, dark area for 24 hours. By this time small shoots should appear. Wash the sprouts before offering them to your pets. The soaked seed and sprouts are especially good for pregnant and baby-rearing mothers.

Animal protein is also beneficial to gerbils. It can be supplied in the form of cheese, milk, boiled eggs, and meat.

Popular Protein Seeds by Constituent %

Seed	Protein	Fat	Carbohydrate	Mineral
Pine Nuts	30	45	12	4
Unsalted Peanuts	25	45	19	5
Linseed	21	35	25	5
Sunflower	20	45	21	3
Rape	20	40	11	6
Hemp	18	32	17	3
Maw	17	40	12	6
Niger	17	32	15	7
Canary Seed	14	6	58	3

While cereal grains are the best food for gerbils, they will eat anything...from lettuce to newspapers. Photo by R. Hanson.

Take care when offering proteins to gerbils. Too much can quickly result in an obese pet. Therefore, feed proteins in small quantities.

GREENFOODS, FRUITS, AND VEGETABLES

All greenfoods and fruits, as well as many root vegetables, are essentially made up of water. They are also rich sources of vitamins and so should be supplied on a regular basis. Introduce greenfoods gradually to young gerbils, and then only in moderate amounts. A glut of greenfood can induce diarrhea.

This food group is enormous. It ranges from the outer leaves of cabbage to dried raisins, from spinach to carrots, and from dandelion to apples. Become familiar with those plants in your locality that a gerbil might enjoy. Plantain, shepherd's purse, and chickweed are all acceptable. Also be aware of which plants may be poisonous. In all cases, the greenfood must be thoroughly washed to remove chemicals and parasites.

Supplying your gerbils with a variety of greenfoods ensures that no vitamins will be lacking. Additionally, this variety will balance the effects of the laxative with

It is easy to provide a good diet for your gerbil. You can purchase seed/grain mixtures that are nutritious and that offer a combination of textures and flavors. Photo courtesy of Hagen.

the effects of the astringent plants.

CALCIUM

Only trace amounts of most minerals are required. These amounts are readily supplied via the various foodstuffs. However, calcium is needed in much larger amounts by pregnant females and growing youngsters. Calcium ensures that the female has sufficient milk for the babies and that the babies have good bone formation. Powdered milk can be sprinkled on cut pieces of fruit, or bread-soaked milk can be given to supplement the calcium requirement.

WATER

Although water is contained in many foods, a supply of fresh water must be available at all times.

Gravity-fed water bottles are the best way to supply your pet with water. They can be readily attached to the side of the cage. Photo courtesy of Hagen.

Water Content by % in Some Popular Foods

Food	Water	Carbohydrate	Protein/Fat
Lettuce	95	2.0	1.2
Carrot	87	9.6	1.21
Dandelion	84	10.6	3.4

AMOUNTS TO FEED

The amount of food needed by your pets can be determined by the quantity of food they consume within a short, given period of time. If large amounts of fruit, greens, or similar products are left in the cage, then you are probably feeding too much. If everything is devoured quickly, then offer a little more. It is normal for a certain amount of food to be stored in a gerbil's nest. Wet foods, such as fruits however, should be removed to prevent the nest from becoming damp. Uneaten fresh foods, particularly those with a high water content, should be removed from the cage after three or four hours. They must not be allowed to sour.

Feed your gerbils at the same time each day. They will soon become accustomed to this schedule and will greet you eagerly. The most important thing to remember when feeding a gerbil is that the basic diet should always be available, supplemented with as much variety as possible. This prevents the development of finicky eaters. Remember, eating habits are acquired at an early age.

Some gerbils are more like mini-pigs. They eat everything. This gerbil is eating toilet-paper rolls. The glue holding the paper together is made of animal byproducts. Photo by Bob Bernhard.

Breeding

This chapter covers breeding purely from a practical standpoint. Genetic theory is discussed in the following chapter.

SEXING

Gerbils can be sexed at about the age of four weeks. By this time, the scrotal sacs of the male are just becoming apparent. Simply hold the gerbil on the palm of your hand. Lift its rear end by holding the root of the tail, leaving the front feet supported on your hand. There is a larger distance between the penis and the anus in the male than that between a female's vaginal opening and anus.

Newly born gerbils are about as big as your thumb. They are born naked. Photo by Paul Bartley.

BREEDING LIFE

The male is capable of breeding for most of its life. The female ceases to breed around the age of two years. By this age, her last litters are likely to be smaller in number and possibly less vigorous. Her best period is between three and fourteen months. Once the female has stopped ovulating, she can be left safely in the company of a male.

BREEDING PROCEDURE

If a male and two females have been reared together from an early age, no introductory procedures are needed. The problem here is that the females will almost certainly become pregnant as soon as they are sexually able. This is too soon for the full growth of the female will

39

Gerbils can be sexed when they are a month old (if you are experienced, that is). There is a greater distance between the penis and anal pore of the male than between the vaginal and anal pores of the female. The gerbil on the right is the male. He is also the more slender of the two.

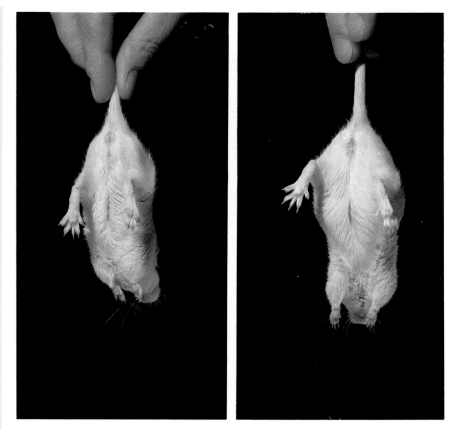

be retarded. Therefore, it is better that breeding operations are delayed by keeping the sexes apart until they are 12-15 weeks old.

A male can be paired with one, two, or three females. He can remain with the females throughout the breeding and rearing period. Male gerbils are good fathers and help rear the youngsters. However, the male will re-

mate with each of the females within a day or so of the female's giving birth. The only way to avoid this is to remove the male sometime before the female is due to give birth to the young.

The female's estrus period is about four or five days. The period between cycles is six days. Gestation averages 23-27 days resulting in a typical litter of five to seven youngsters. The gestation period of females re-mated after the birth of the first litter is extended. The reason is that the fertilized eggs will not be implanted in the uterus until the first litter is ready to be weaned. This process is known as delayed implantation. It is seen in a number of animal forms.

A good procedure is to place the female(s) in a special breeding cage with a mesh divider about mid-way. The male is placed in the other section. Remove the divider after 24 hours. The male will approach the female. As neither has a territorial advantage, fighting is less likely.

Mating usually takes place in the hours of darkness. It is preceded by much chasing of the female by the male. When she is sexually ready, she allows the male to mate her. He will do this several times within a short period.

If this introduction does not go smoothly and there is a lot of fighting, simply separate the pair by replacing the mesh. Try again in a few days. If it fails again, try a new mate. Females are usually cooperative, particularly in the company

of other females.

The advantage of pairing a male with two females at the same time is should one female die, refuse to rear her offspring, or become ill, the babies can then be fostered by the other mother. The young can also be fostered by any other mother with young of similar age.

The gerbils should have a good supply of nesting material so they can make snug nests for their babies. Once a female is pregnant, do not handle her at all unless absolutely essential. Likewise, once the young are born, leave the nest undisturbed other than to have a quick peek while the mother is out. Do not touch the babies. Your scent may stress the female into killing or deserting her offspring.

This newborn gerbil litter contains 5 individuals, all born naked. Photo by Michael Gilroy.

THE BIRTH

Gerbils are born blind and quite helpless. However, they grow rapidly. Their eyes open any time after the eighth day, and are fully open in about 10 to 12 days. Fur grows almost immediately. Within seven days they should have a thin covering of hair.

Gerbil mothers are extremely attentive to their babies. They wash their young continually. This induces the babies to defecate. Any youngsters that inadvertently crawl out of the nest are promptly brought back. The fathers are as diligent as the mother in helping to rear the offspring. In this sense, they can be compared to guinea pigs.

Occasionally, a less-than-good mother is encountered. There is often a good reason for this. It may be that she was too young to have a

Two doves and a cinnamon gerbil ten days old and still with unopened eyes. Photo by Michael Gilroy.

litter, was not well, or was underfed. Sometimes a stressed female kills her babies if she thinks conditions are exceedingly less than ideal. In such a case, make notes on her breeding card. Determine if there is a reason for her not attending to her duties and correct it if possible. If all seems well, it could be an inherent characteristic. Do not use her again for breeding if this is the case. Sometimes a female kills one or two of her litter, but rears the rest with no problem. Mothers have an inborn ability to sense if something is wrong with a baby and may kill it if it is ill. It would also be quite common if she then devoured the baby.

The same trio as on the facing page, 20 days after birth. The pups are now about ready for weaning. Photo by Michael Gilroy.

43

FOSTERING

It may be necessary to foster out the baby gerbils. This is best done when the parents are out of the nest. Pick up the scent of the foster parents by rubbing their urine-stained nesting material on your hands. Then rub your hands over the bodies of the youngsters so the new parents will not reject them. Things normally progress smoothly. If not, remove the young and rub more of the foster parents' scent onto them.

WEANING

Converting a baby from a milk diet to solid foods is called weaning. This is normally completed around the age of 21 days. During the build-up period, supply small mashes of softfood composed of milk-soaked bread with maybe some cheese and seeds added. By 30 days of age, the gerbils can be separated from their parents and split into two sex groups.

If a male is to be re-introduced into a former colony, wipe him with the urine dust from the colony pen. The members may have forgotten his scent and could attack him. Re-introduction is not a problem if done with care and supervision.

A black mother and her Canadian White Spot offspring. The pups are about 8 days old. They are two weeks away from being weaned from a liquid to a solid diet. Photo by Michael Gilroy.

44

BREEDING METHODS

Only fit gerbils are to be used for breeding. Using inferior gerbils invites all sorts of problems. Gerbils with known defects should not be bred. If any bad faults appear in the line, attempt to trace the defective individuals to remove them from the program. This is where breeding records prove so useful. Each gerbil has its own information card. The card records which gerbils have been mated to which, how many young were born, how many survived, any abnormalities, the colors, etc. The more information included, the easier it is to determine the good and bad producers.

Once you have purchased your initial breeding stock, it is best that no new stock be added unless it comes from the same line of gerbils. If you find that breeding is for you, purchase a second trio, or just two more females (unrelated to the other females) if your male is a really good specimen. He can be mated to both pairs of females. This way you have two strains underway, with the common factor of the male.

You need to be adept at selecting the finest youngsters from these two lines. Initially, inbreed them to their father, mother, brother, or sister to fix the best points. The faults likewise will be fixed, but at least they will show up early in your program. By careful selection of your retained stock, breed only from those not displaying these faults. As long as you stay within your own gene lines each generation should steadily improve.

Should problems become evident, they can probably be rectified by the introduction of a second strain related in a mild form; it will be a good outcross. Once a few generations have been bred, it is essential that you do not suddenly introduce unknown genes to your stock by using a gerbil about which you know very little. This could rapidly undo much of the progress you have made.

After the initial inbreeding, you will conduct a more dilute form of breeding referred to as linebreeding; gerbils that are more distantly related are mated. These gerbils still

carry a good percent of the genes of the original male or female whose features you planned to build on. The key to successful breeding is your ability to retain the best gerbils.

BREEDING UNITS

The essentials of a breeding room are that it is free from drafts, vermin proof, and well-ventilated. Ideally it will have electric and water facilities. Some stout shelving is needed to support the weight of the gerbil cages. Adequate storage facilities are required for the extra food and equipment. A number of spare cages is a must, as is a hospital cage complete with an infra-red lamp, thermometer, and thermostatic regulator. A work bench is useful for planning matings and conducting regular health checks on the stock.

Another useful addition is an ionizer. This simply plugs into an electrical socket to release millions of negative ions. These ions attract and weigh down dust and bacteria. The particles are removed from the air and

A male gerbil mounts a receptive female preparatory to mating. The female is dove colored and the male is an agouti Canadian White.

47

deposited on the floor and other surfaces. They are easily wiped away. Hence, the spread of infection is greatly reduced.

It is advisable to cover all windows with a fine mesh. During warm weather, the windows can be opened for fresh air without the risk of predators entering. Likewise, ventilation ducts, both high and low in the room, should be covered with the mesh.

A low output heater makes it more comfortable for you to work during cooler weather. Keep the temperature low, for high temperatures increase bacterial reproduction rates. Keep it just sufficient to take the chill out of the air.

Identical brown agouti parents are predictably throwing off brown agouti pups.

Genetics

A breeder immediately benefits in two ways with just a basic understanding of the principles governing heredity. First, the result of pairings can be predicted with great certainty. Second, knowing how features are transmitted means that you can influence or correct breeding results.

This chapter explains the simplest genetic principles. A progression to more complex aspects can be pursued by the interested reader. The subject is really quite fascinating.

GENES

Inherent traits are transmitted from one generation to the next by minute bodies of coded information known as genes. Each species has thousands of these genes. They control (over statement) both physical and behavioral traits.

Genes are arranged like beads on a thread. The thread is the chromosome. In each body cell, there are numerous chromosome pairs. One of each pair is received from each parent. The chromosomes are, for all practical purposes, identical to each other in length. Each gene has its opposite gene for a given feature, whether this be for hair color, head size, ear shape, etc. The feature may be controlled by a single pair of genes or, more typically, controlled by many pairs along the chromosome length.

As an animal grows, the chromosomes divide along their length to create chromatids. One chromatid of each pair moves to one end of the cell while its alternate chromatid moves to the other end. The cell then divides. Thus a new daughter cell is formed containing a pair of chromosomes identical to those from which it came. This process is repeated many times as an animal grows.

The exception to this identical paired rule is found in the sex cells. Here the chromosomes differ in length. The longer of the two is the X. The shorter is the Y. A male has an X and a Y; a female has two X chromosomes.

REPRODUCTION

If each parent passed on both of its chromosomes, then the number of chromosome pairs would double at each new generation. This does not happen because the sex cells divide differently than other body cells.

The chromosomes divide into chromatids as before. Then, chromatids of a similar pair twist around each other. Next they separate, or 'cross over.' During this 'crossing over,' some of the genes from one chromatid exchange places with those on their opposite chromatid.

The chromatids then polarize. Thus two cells are formed from one. At the next cell division, the chromosomes move to opposite ends of the cell. The cell divides. The new cells have only one chromosome from an original pair. These become the gametes (sperm or ova) depending on their sex. When these unite with the gametes of the other parent,

the zygote formed has the normal pairs of chromosomes. A new generation has been created.

PURITY OF GENES

For our purposes, we'll assume that a single gene controls color. Then it can easily be demonstrated that each parent contributes a gene for color on the chromosome they pass to their offspring. Either the genes are for the same color or they are for different colors. If for the same color, the youngsters are homozygous, or purebreeding, for that color. If the genes are for differing colors, the young are heterozygous, or nonpure, for color. Any feature can be substituted for color; the calculations and theory remain the same. Color is just a simple example to use.

If two purebreeding agouti gerbils are mated, all the young will be agouti since no other genes could be passed to the offspring. However, if an agouti is mated to an albino, what is the result? The answer is that all of the youngsters will look agouti. This is known as their phenotype. However, they will carry, or be 'split' for, the albino gene. If these 'split' youngsters are paired, they will produce purebreeding agoutis, non-purebreeding agoutis, and purebreeding albinos in the ratio of 1:2:1. Let's take a

look at this in terms of the genetic make-up, or genotype of the gerbils.

SYMBOLS

Letters will be symbols for the genes in this analysis. The agouti gene is "A" and the albino is "a." In purebreeding agoutis, the gene each parent passes to its offspring is 'A.' The babies are thus AA. In purebreeding albinos, each parent passes on an 'a.' Therefore the youngsters have a genotype of aa. If these two types are paired, the agouti can pass on only

an 'A,' while the albino can pass on only 'a.' The babies must have a genotype of Aa.

The reason the progeny look agouti is because some genes are more potent than others; these are called dominants. Others are less potent; these are called recessives. In effect, the dominant gene masks the recessive gene's appearance, yet the latter is still present. This is written as agouti/albino. The color before the slash is the visual color; the latter is masked. This example refers to agouti split for albino.

The dominant colors are placed in capital letters. Recessives are set in lower case. When written, it is seen that there are two types of agouti: AA, which is purebreeding, or homozygous, and Aa, which is non-pure breeding, or heterozygous. Both look exactly the same, but their genetic make-up differs.

When the non-pure agoutis pair with each other, each parent can pass on either its 'A' gene or its 'a' gene, but not both. This means that the permutations are AA, Aa, aA, and aa. (There is no difference between Aa and

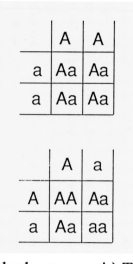

aA—both are agouti.) The
result is the 1:2:1 ratio
already mentioned. Notice
that in order to be seen
visually, the albinos must
have both their genes for this
color. In other words,
recessive must be in double
dose to be visual, while
dominants need to be only in
single dose.

RANDOM   SELECTION

This precise result of such
a mating happens only in
theory. The calculations of
genetic principles work out
over large numbers, but not
necessarily in one or even a
few matings. In reality, all
agoutis, all albinos, or other
permutations could result
from the mating in the given
example. The more litters,
the nearer the numbers come

to the expected calculations.

How do we know which
traits are dominant and
which are recessive? Initially,
we don't. This is discovered
over a period of time
through many pairings.
From these, geneticists can
determine the recessive from
the dominant. When a new
mutation appears, breeders
mate it with any other colors
available and record the
results. Through this a
picture begins to emerge as
to how it is transmitted.

SEX
DETERMINATION

The sex of a gerbil is
controlled by the male. He
can pass on either an X or a
Y chromosome. The female
can pass on only an X. She
has no alternative. In theory,
there is a 50/50 chance of
either sex being produced.
There are sex limiting
factors, though, which can
come into play. The result is
a higher proportion of one
sex, depending on the
species.

SEX   LINKAGE

It sometimes happens that
a feature appears on the X
chromosome, but, because
the Y is shorter, there is no

Mating gerbils.
The contact is
very fleeting.
Photo by Michael
Gilroy.

corresponding gene. Indeed, the Y chromosome appears to be concerned solely with matters of sexual differences between the animals. When such a trait is sex-linked, it no longer needs to be in double dose to show itself in the male. This is particularly applicable to recessives. It also has interest in the case of dominants because it means that if the male exhibits the feature there is no question of whether or not it is split or pure for its color; a sex-linked feature cannot be split in the male. Whatever is visual is regarded as pure.

The female, however, can be split for a sex-linked trait. For example, in the case of our agouti x albino mating, the offspring could be AA or Aa. This would not be possible if agouti was sex-linked (the male would be either A or a.) In the example, only a series of test matings would establish which agoutis were pure and which were non-pure. This could be costly in terms of time, space, feeding, and rearing the litters. Were agouti sex-linked, any males would be purebreeding for the color they exhibited,

regardless of whether agouti was dominant or recessive.

POLYGENIC ACTION

Breeders are concerned with more than just one trait. They are interested in the overall way their gerbils look and behave. Here things become rather complex because a great number of genes control all the characteristics of an animal. What makes matters even more difficult is that we do not know whether desirable genes are better in their pure or their heterozygous state. We'll look at polygenic action with a view to pointing out a few important aspects that can create problems both when selecting stock and when trying to improve it. For this discussion, assume that all desirable features are purebreeding dominants and that undesirable features are recessive.

If six pairs of genes control the entire form of our gerbils, then one having the genotype of AABBCCDDEEFF will be a superb looking animal. Unfortunately, so will AaBbCcDdEeFf. The difference is that the former can pass on only good qualities, while the latter can pass on any combination of good and bad. Furthermore, regardless of the quality of its mate, the first gerbil's offspring will still look good. In the second gerbil's case, much depends on the genotype of its mate.

An average gerbil is AaBBccDdEEff or a similar permutation with some good features, some bad, some purebreeding, and others not. Since we cannot differentiate between the first super purebreeding and the super non-purebreeder, we should evaluate the stock of the two breeders. The chances are that the overall stock quality of the first breeder will be high, having achieved such a true breeding gerbil. The quality of the second breeder will be considerably more varied. This would account for its more heterogenous state. In other words, the uniformity of stock is the strongest indicator that the qualities of a good looking gerbil will breed true.

Breeding potential cannot be judged solely from the sight of one outstanding winner at a show. Back home, the breeder could have a stud full of inferior specimens. The winner was just a matter of luck, not breeding expertise. An understanding of genetics explains how such winners happen to come along.

Regardless of its pedigree, a gerbil that looks like rubbish will breed rubbish. A poor specimen may have a genotype of AabbccDdeeff. It does not have much of value to pass onto its offspring. Chances are that many of them will not even receive the A or D. It really comes down to how good its mate is. When breeding, a lot of poor specimens will be produced. Only by removing these and retaining the best is stock steadily improved.

If we had a gerbil of AABBCCddEEFF, we need only a single D to produce DD down the line. By acquiring a gerbil good for D, we are likely to acquire a different fault in that same gerbil. So in correcting one fault, another is introduced. This fault may not show itself for a generation or two. This is why we must stay within our own strain. Outcrosses must be introduced with considerable

care; test mate them for more than one generation to see the full effect they will have on your established stock.

Of course, a gerbil's features are controlled by many more pairs of genes than six. It must also be appreciated that an undesired feature may be linked with a new color mutation or hair type. This means that, as we breed to improve color, the fault is intensified. In such cases, the hope is that the fault will separate at some point. The color can then be improved without increasing the occurrence of the fault, which can be selectively bred out of the strain.

THE NON-GENETIC ASPECT

Simply because a gerbil has the gene potential to be a good breeder does not make its appearance so. Genes are affected by the environment as much as by other genes in the animal. For example, if a gerbil is fed incorrectly, it may exhibit retarded growth. This complicates matters because a gerbil may look less than superb, yet have the ability to pass on potential quality. Therefore, applying genetic theory goes hand in hand with sound husbandry.

Albinos, when mated, can produce only albinos.

Diseases and First Aid

The best way to cope with health problems is to avoid them in the first place! Of course, even in the best run stockrooms, illness and accidents can occur. But with good husbandry, problems are less likely to happen. And when misfortune does present itself, it is more easily pinpointed and eradicated. Personally examine your stock each day. The earlier an ailment is detected, the easier it is to treat.

Incubation: Many people introduce new gerbils into an established colony without a period of quarantine. This is inviting disaster. If the new gerbil is harboring an illness, the disease will rapidly spread throughout the entire stock.

Regardless of their source, newly acquired gerbils must spend a minimum of 14 days in isolation. The quarantine quarters should be as far from the rest of the stock as possible. During this time, monitor the new additions, and check that they are eating well and that no signs of illness appear. If all is well after two weeks, introduce them into the colony.

Likewise, exhibition stock should not be returned directly to the stockroom. They may have been exposed to a variety of ailments at the competition.

Isolating the gerbil is the most important thing to do at the first sign of illness. Separating the diseased animal from the rest of the stock inhibits the spread of contamination.

Cleanliness: Food and water containers must not only be refilled every day but they must also be washed. Additionally, the pots and other accessories must always be returned to the same cage. Transfer of such items among the cages invites the spread of parasites and disease.

Hospital Cage: An ill gerbil should be placed in a hospital cage. This is simply a cage or fish tank with a heat source, such as an infra-red lamp, light bulb, or heating pad. A thermometer indicates the level of heat, which should be about 22°C (72°F). The heat source should be placed at one end of the hospital cage so that the gerbil can move to and from the heat as desired. Often isolation and a heat source are all that are required to cure a sick gerbil. Be sure food and plenty of water are always available.

Keep the gerbil confined to the hospital cage until recovery is complete. Gradually reduce the temperature over two or three days before returning the gerbil to its customary accommodations.

Abscess: Due to an insect or a bite from another gerbil, swelling may develop. Periodically bathe the area gently with a mild antiseptic. The swelling may go down or it may grow and burst. If the swelling does not disappear, it may be a more serious tumor. Consult a vet.

Colds: Causes are many, but colds are typically due to a drafty situation. Gerbils most likely affected are those recovering from an illness or those in less than fit condition. The nose and eyes may produce a discharge; the bowels may be more viscous than normal; sometimes, the gerbil has a hunched look and the fur does not lay close to the body.

Place the gerbil in a hospital cage. Maintain a temperature around 22°C (72°F). Offer only dry food and water. Recovery should be rapid. If not, consult a vet.

Diarrhea: Often diarrhea is not an isolated complaint, but a symptom of another infection. It is the result of internal reactions within the body. Mild looseness in the droppings may be merely the result of an excess of greenfood. Whatever the cause may be, isolate the gerbil and remove or reduce the quantity of greenfood until the condition improves. Do not purchase antibiotics without the advice of a vet.

External Parasites: Rodents are remarkably free of fleas. In fact, external parasites on rodents often indicate poor attention to cage cleaning. Lice, mites, and fleas can also be transmitted via contact with other animals.

Lice are small, grayish creatures that spend their

entire life on a host. They are usually found near the neck or rump. They move slowly in the fur and lay their eggs on the hair follicles. Lice suck the blood of their host.

Mites, like lice, also suck the blood of their host. Mites, however, invade their host during nighttime hours. They hide in crevices during the day. As a result, mites are more difficult than lice to spot and treat.

A build–up of external parasites can seriously affect the health of gerbils. Sleep is lost due to constant scratching. Babies can become anemic and die. This is one of the reasons that good hygiene is so crucial.

The treatment of all external parasites is the same. Obtain a suitable acaricide from your vet or petshop. Infected animals and their cages require repeated applications to kill newly hatched parasites. All bedding material should be burned and other cage accessories sterilized.

Fur and Skin: Gerbils secrete an oil which they groom onto their coats. This oil evaporates in the wild. If your gerbils have a greasy look to them, it is because the atmosphere is too humid; the oil cannot evaporate. Either relocate your gerbils or reduce the humidity.

Bald patches may be created by the continual scratching of parasites. If the parasites appear like small rings and become encrusted, suspect ringworm. This is not really a worm but a fungal infection. Once established, it is difficult to totally remove. All bedding must be burned and the cages blowtorched. Consult a vet for medication.

A reddened area with missing fur may indicate that a gerbil is chewing at its own fur; another member of the group may also be the culprit. The problem is often one of overcrowding, boredom, or some other stressful situation. Correct the situation if possible.

Heatstroke: A gerbil exposed to strong sunlight may suffer from heat stroke. The animal will lie still and may pant. Remove the gerbil to a cool, quiet spot. Place a damp cloth over its body to gradually lower its temperature.

Malocclusion: When the front teeth are not aligned properly, they are not worn down by the gnawing action. The teeth continue to grow unchecked, either outside or inside the gerbil's mouth. The cause may have been a nutritional deficiency while the gerbil was young or a genetic weakness. Do not breed a gerbil exhibiting this genetic defect. The situation must be monitored or the gerbil eventually may not be able to eat. A vet can trim the teeth periodically.

Sterility: If more and more of your gerbils are sterile (not because of old age), the cause may be in your breeding program. Infertility can also be created by nutritional deficiency. Introduce a gerbil with a proven record of high fertility to your breeding stud. Always breed with due consideration for unseen characteristics. Again, detailed breeding records are so important.

You can just look at a gerbil, when you have experience, and be fairly certain that it is healthy and well cared for. Photo by Burkhard Kahl.

Exhibitions

The exhibition of gerbils is both exciting and entertaining. It may lead to new friendships, as it is as much a special occasion as it is a competition. All the gerbil colors will be on view, together with any new varieties that have been established.

Your show gerbils need to be presented in the cleanest possible state. A special cage is not required for certain classes, such as those for children. These less strict classes encourage newcomers to participate. A standard exhibition cage is a must for more serious exhibitions.

ENTERING SHOWS

The best way to find out about future shows is to visit one in your area. Your petshop may know of one, or can put you in touch with an exhibitor. It is certainly worthwhile to join a local gerbil club or small animal society. Membership in a national gerbil club makes you eligible for any special cups or prizes offered at the exhibition.

Once you know about an upcoming show, apply for a schedule from the show secretary of the event. The schedule details the various classes at that particular show. These vary depending on the number of exhibits anticipated. The schedule indicates the regulations governing the classes. This includes things such as the sex of the gerbil, its color, and whether or not it previously has won any first prizes. If you wish to enter an exhibit, complete the form and return it with any entry fees. You will receive labels to place on the show cage, along with any other necessary instructions.

SHOW PREPARATION

Gerbils are judged against the national society's official standard. You will be supplied with a description of this standard if you join the society.

Well before the show date, you must begin to prepare the gerbil. Every day the gerbil should be placed into a small cage similar to the show cage. It should be left there for increasingly longer periods of time.

Index

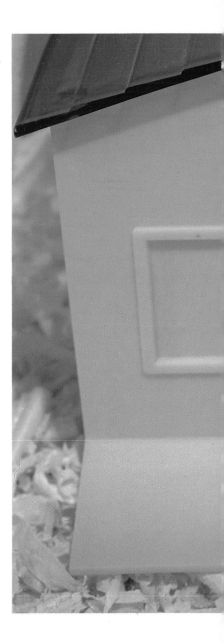